He's a Color Until He's Not

He's a Color Until He's Not

poems
by Christian Hanz Lozada

He's a Color Until He's Not
© Copyright 2023 Christian Hanz Lozada
All rights reserved. No part of this book may be used or reproduced in any manner whatsoever without written permission from either the author or the publisher, except in the case of credited epigraphs or brief quotations embedded in articles or reviews.

Editor-in-chief
Eric Morago

Editor Emeritus
Michael Miller

Marketing Specialist
Ellen Webre

Proofreader
LeAnne Hunt

Front cover art
Christian Hanz Lozada

Author photo
Lessa Pelato-Lozada

Book design
Michael Wada

Moon Tide logo design
Abraham Gomez

He's a Color Until He's Not
is published by Moon Tide Press

Moon Tide Press
6709 Washington Ave. #9297
Whittier, CA 90608
www.moontidepress.com

FIRST EDITION

Printed in the United States of America

ISBN # 987-1-957799-14-8

Further Praise for *He's a Color Until He's Not*

With sharp insight, Lozada chisels the binary of White and Brown. From bango tags and rock gardens to epistles and song, he gives shape to the liminal zone where histories of hate and fear have rendered us monsters. There, Lozada works outside in by showing us Monster watching, navigating, longing, and loving—all in colors unbound.

— Jade Hidle, author of *The Return to Viet Nam*.

Digging into Christian Hanz Lozada's latest collection is like conducting a séance. In this book you will be met with many spirits: the ghosts of childhood; the ghosts of video game gods; the ghosts of racism; the ghost of Bukowski; and the specter of imperialism. Reader, what I'm trying to tell you is that these poems are haunting--they will confront you and stay with you. Light a candle and rejoice that good poetry is alive and thriving.

— Nikolai Garcia, author of *Nuclear Shadows of Palm Trees*

Christian Hanz Lozada brings race and ethnicity to center stage and demands our attention. His words spare no feelings as he illustrates the bias, racism, and double standards often afforded in excess to people of color and brings to life the agony and ecstasy of being mixed race. His poetry pushes us to do better, to check our privilege by the first page, and challenges us to see the world through the eyes of a Filipino-American longing for home in a country determined to segregate and discriminate.

— Mauricio "Soul on Fire" Moreno, author of *Anatomy of a Flame*

For anyone who grows up loving but not having the vocabulary to express it.

For Lessa, I guess, but I didn't need to write it.

Maybe Steve, too, because he won't leave.

And for Romee, who, in our next life, will steal the money when I tell her to.

Contents

Further Praise for He's a Color Until He's Not ... 5
The Hook in Your Mouth ... 13

Part 1: Planted Where Thorns Grow

Letter 1 by White Aunt ... 16
The Assignment: Describe Your Family's Migration Story ... 17
Home Movies ... 18
23 and Me (Monster) ... 19
A Living and Hateful Silence ... 20
Twenty Unasked Questions in ... 21
White Grandfather's Absence ... 21
Racist Rules Can Keep You Safe ... 22
Childhood Games ... 23
California Sun ... 24
The Wrong Kind of Bitter ... 26
Monster Learns to Love ... 27
Using Chinatown to Converse with Brown Dad ... 29
Miracle Meat ... 30
Addition by Subtraction ... 31
There Is a Call If You Can Hear It ... 32
Chasing a Happy Memory ... 33
Gods of the Liquor Store Video Game ... 34
Like Tanked Sharks, We Circle and Bump ... 35
The Genetic Memory of a Hawk ... 36
Give Me a Dumb Dog ... 37
There Are Rules ... 38

Part 2: How to Make an Asian American

Letter 2 by White Aunt ... 42
Buried Family History ... 43
Clarinet Shrieks Raise the Dead ... 44
Mixed-Race Tax ... 45
Every Other Word Is Silence: A Broken Pantoum ... 46
White Not-Cousin in Tennessee Reads Her Ancestry ... 47

Holidays Are Hurricanes	48
We Internalize It Young	49
The Reason for the Shirk	50
Monster Imagines the Surgery	51
I Stopped Drawing Because of a White Girl	52
How to Clean Unhealing Wounds	53
The Calculus of Help and Hope	54
The Emotionally Orphaned Search for Traditions	56
Like a burlap bag of possum babies	58

Part 3: Migration Means Always Being Haunted, and Returning Means Giving Ghosts Substance

Letter 3 by White Aunt	62
The New Rules	63
Evergreen Bowling Lanes	64
Movie Theater Summer Camp	65
Filipinx Crab Mentality	66
Word Problems	67
If you ask if I speak Tagalog	68
When the Invasive Becomes Domestic	69
The Desert Tortoise Is New	70
The stories are in the gaps and the silences	71
Bury It When You Land	72
This Year We'll Try Color	74
When Trapped	75
The Travel Tax	76
Filling Cebu with My Last Breath	77
The Rot Is on the Inside	78
While My Veins Thicken, While My Heart Pounds	79
My Place in Kingsport, Tennessee	80
That Soothing Warmth and The Pressure	81
Made in the Image	82

Part 4: Touching From A Distance

Letter 4 by White Aunt	84
You Know What You Did	85
I Presented My Writing at The Twin Towers Correctional Facility	86
Fishing in Dirty Water	87
White Grandma called to warn me	88
The Bullets That Were Close to Me	89
Gatekeepers Create a Mission Statement	90
Death Shouldn't Be Time for Selfishness	91
All Brown Dad Has	92
Deathbed Love Languages	93
Just a Cardboard Box with a Label	94
House Keeping	95
The Bukowskis Went Transcendental	96
White Math	97
A Fulcrum Increasing Leverage and Blood	98
Living in Red	100

Part 5: Please, Oh Please, Be Untouched by Trauma A Little Longer

Dear White Aunt,	102
Dear Sherman 1	103
Dear Sherman 2	104
Dear Sherman 3	105
Dear Sherman 4	106
It Is Barren	107
The Village of Fathers	108
Manspreading Can Go So Far	109
Crafting	110
Portrait of a Bench in New Zealand	111
Maybe Life Is Better When	112
That Old Scam	114
Hoping for Hanai	115
The Breath of a House	116
The Talk Is an Ongoing Dialogue	118
I Say, I Say	119

Use the Debris to Build	120
Glossary of Terms or How to Read *a Christian Hanz Lozada Poem*	*121*
Afterforeword by Steven Hendrix	*123*
About the Author	*125*
Acknowledgments	*126*

The Hook in Your Mouth

The hook in your mouth, when it sinks in,
pulls you through the scent of want—
to the things you refuse to see.

My bait is undesirable and dangerous.
I start poems with words like *White* and *Brown*,
centered and capitalized colors.

That moment you're racialized is the hook's point,
burrowed into the corner of your mouth and controlling
your tongue or swallowed and hung up on guts.

You can feel the internal bleeding of the powerless,
reeled in one direction, measured, skinned, and eaten.
I call it Wednesday.

But the hook isn't the point, and the poem isn't the words.
And you, the smart White reader, can still slip by
discerning the difference between racism's rot

and the infantilized foreign, can avoid the traps
and never see, which is how privilege cuts,
after all.

Part 1:
PLANTED WHERE THORNS GROW

Letter 1 by White Aunt

Jan 5, 1972
Dear Momma + Daddy,

I'm all mixed up.
You tell me that I'm too fond of n------
when I hang around over at Carol's
you say they are the wrong type
of people.

What sort of people do you want me to like?

I know you are doing it for my own good
I had to get away
think things over.
I was debating on leaving home.
But I love you two too much
If I leave, it's only for a while
I'll
       be
            back.
Carol has respect for both of you, but I lie and tell her a lie.
Don't call the pigs if I leave cause
I'll
       be
            back.

The Assignment:
Describe Your Family's Migration Story

Monster left school excited by the stories he'd hear,
but the assignment didn't require a narrative
in a language the teacher understood.

He thought he'd write the Brown side,	He thought he'd write the White side,
the many moves from island to island,	not the migration from Europe
country to country, then here.	but from the South to the West.
He asked Brown Dad,	He asked White Mom,
he asked his manoy,	he asked White Grandma,
and they described shame	and both described loss
through slaps and belts.	through red-flushed tears.

When classmates passed their papers forward,
Monster took the stack from the kid behind him,
lowered his head, added nothing. Given the task
to document competing selves the boy
chose to erase, erase, erase.

Home Movies

Brown Uncle bought guns from mixed-race kids back home—
off-base children of shipped-out fathers and angry mothers.
He'd hide the important pieces from customs in car parts,
like reverse balikbayan boxes, and rebuilt rifles to loan or sell

to cousins and coworkers. Monster's 6-year-old bones
still rattled after a day shooting army surplus at junk cars,
refrigerators, and mannequins. Afterward, he and his brothers
would paper rock scissors; losers hid under the blanket in back,

held their breath until drive-thru admission was paid.
After parking and deep inhalations, the family would watch,
all the Apocalypses, Platoons, Metal Jackets, and MIAs.
At the start of every one, Brown Dad would whisper:

"This was filmed in the Philippines."

Monster's mind would light up like a tracer round.
US invasion was like flipping through family photos,
Vietnam stories became home movies of the Jeeps
his father was born with, of the guns they just shot,
of the cousins left behind.

23 and Me (Monster)

Brown genes are not a story:　　White genes are not a story:
　　　　Asian migration,　　　　Euro migration,
　　　　　hopping islands,　　　　hopping an ocean,
　a colonizer's extended stay,　　resting White feet on Black necks,
　　　　　　mostly Filipino　　　mostly White

　　　　　but for one Black ancestor
　　　　　　around 1700-1800

Negligibly Other means　　　Negligibly Black means
　　having dark blood,　　　having a secret,
　　means almost pure;　　　dirty and well-kept,
　one more generation　　　but in the keeping,
　　to bleach blemishes,　　what we lose are the stories
　　to erase us before.　　　and, possibly, love.

　　　Without the stories, it's all hate,
　　　　　hate and, probably,
　　　　more unspeakable things.

A Living and Hateful Silence

Some days I give him the finger as I pass,
ignoring his oil-based receding hairline,
the one that has been at low tide
since our twenties.

Other days, I drop my eyes,
not seeing his weird but natural
sun-and-dirt-stained skin on canvas pores,
shades of non-sequitur reds and browns
like a non-existent Cherokee ancestor
trying to speak through our flesh.

And still other days, I embrace the silence
lingering around his brushed on blue-eyed gaze,
like the one dinner we shared.
I sat on one end; he sat on the other,
and we talked only to those whose blood
was similarly hued. Never to each other.

White Grandfather stares at my homecoming.
His brow, like mine, rolls forward
over his eyes and dips deep in the center,
frozen there, above the fireplace,
hovering over the bricks
covered in white, oil-based paint.
I try to mirror his actions,
the ones that mean the most: every day,
for decades, pretend he doesn't exist
and hate that red-brown skin.

Twenty Unasked Questions in White Grandfather's Absence

1. If your pickup line for an orphan is the promise of family, how can you leave?

2. How deep is your love for a daughter doubled over and crying?

3. How deep did your skin split from punching her?

4. Could you feel the Black skin she loved and you hated through your fists?

5. How proud are you of your two-job teen drowning in a Black school, saving up for a White, private escape but spending it all on her twice-orphaned mother?

6. Why do you only talk to the son who strapped his future on the child inside his girlfriend?

7. Isn't 15 too young to be a father?

8. Why didn't you chase your addict son who spent more time on the street than at home?

9. Why won't you acknowledge me?
10. Why won't you acknowledge me?
11. Why won't you acknowledge me?
12. Why won't you acknowledge me?
13. Why won't you acknowledge me?
14. Why won't you acknowledge me?
15. Why won't you acknowledge me?
16. Why won't you acknowledge me?
17. Why won't you acknowledge me?
18. Why won't you acknowledge me?
19. Why won't you acknowledge me?
20. Why won't you acknowledge me?

Racist Rules Can Keep You Safe

Monster remembers wanting with the others,
the Darker Thans, for something other than
a makeshift tetherball made of a grocery bag,
a soccer ball, a no parking sign, and a patch of sharp,
too-short-this-month-to-water-brown grass.

He remembers following the rules and coming home
before dark, taking the ball--that mark between wanting
and more want--with him. The others lined up
along the fence and pelted him, then the house, with rocks.
Tack, tack, tack, tack, tack, tack, tack

thundered want against the walls.
When a storm rages outside, best to hunker
and wait. When it passes, know not to stray
because weather is cyclical, and butterfly wings
keep getting beat.

Childhood Games

White Grandma and I didn't play games
like Pattycake, I Spy, or Hot Hands.
Instead, we would play our own game, Big Eyes.
The rules were simple: White Grandma would say,
"Make big eyes for me," and I did.
"Bigger," and I did until my eyes would water
and she would laugh, and I would lose.

California Sun

White Grandma loves to watch me eat fruit,
especially the fruit she has given me. She marvels
at the piecemeal peeling of oranges and absolute
daring to bite through the skin of an apple
with the confidence of natural teeth, filled cavities,
and impatience. For her, fruit either takes time or sacrifice.
It takes up your space, your water, your sun or your
adopted daddy saving his money, newspapers,
and Sears Catalogs to purchase an orange for each child
and wrap the fruit in faraway stories and impossible dreams.

On holidays, as the paper was torn away, the California sun
would glow through the cracks and shine
when completely revealed. White Grandma would savor
each slice, for days if she could, but for hours.
There were no presents but a bit more pork, a bit more sugar,
a bit more baking, a bit more love and edible sunshine.
For me, fruit either takes a trip to the market or cash enough
to roll down my window and buy ten pounds of sunshine
at any corner. The tinted plastic around each glowing orb
uniformed their color and size and clumped this cosmos

close enough to promise I could eat them all.
On any day of the week, I open the bag and let a ball
or two spill out, one in my hand, the others wherever,
and I eat the slices like popcorn—mindless and repetitive
but for those rare moments I think of Arturo Bandini
subsisting on them solely till even the rats stopped
coming around or remember White Grandma and the absolute
joy and pride at having separated some of her pay or social
security
for this little ray of her childhood and Southern days
practically placed on my tongue like the body of Christ.

In those moments, I can taste the water and the sun
and the salty dirt that gets trapped beneath fingernails

and in the creases and wrinkles of working joints.
The sweetness of each pulpy cell is heightened by
the bitterness of soil and the saltiness of sweat.

The Wrong Kind of Bitter

White Grandma's addiction is three pots a day,
Folgers. By my math, it's 40 years of no good
and never right. When we go out, I keep her addiction
in mind and log her slurp reactions. When she sighs
and curls crooked fingers around the mug, soaking
some joy through easily-torn skin, I ask, "Good?"
"That's about right." I ask, "What does right taste like?"
In country logic, with a slurped sigh, she says, "this coffee."

After a success, we repeat a week later, have the same
everything. When she sips and her always-scowl deepens,
I ask, "What does wrong taste like?" "Blech," she answers.
"It's bitter and never good." And we migrate the next week,
going from cup to cup and place to place, all of them greased
as if one plate too many was served before a scrubbing,
like a table after Thanksgiving, cleared but not clean.

I watch White Grandma's knuckle-swollen fingers trace
a cup's handle, grounding her in that feeling of overused
plates and lip smudges. I want those moments when strange
alchemy bridges boiling water and beans to a contented
gesture. I want to give White Grandma the magic that links
the orphaning drunk to the shoe-giving daddy,
that links the sneering-smiled husband and her babies
to the weight of her second
man, a young immigrant stitched to her side, that links
the moment she cut the thread to the third husband who said
"stop shoveling shit against the tide," and that link
to the absence whose absence comes in waves.
I search for something to cut through her shades of bitterness
where every cup is wrong and where right lasts for a few sips.

Monster Learns to Love

I. White Grandma

Her pale hands are horror-movie branches scratching
Monster's windows that cast shadows across your wall
reaching for him. She wants to touch him, hold him close,
with her gnarled-wood fingers, and he flinches every time
because he can feel her fear and want in them.

And because he flinches, White Grandma shows love
in the only way she knows: cleaning. She'll clean his floors,
wash his clothes, soak everything in bleach
as if using her hospital-housekeeping skills to cover up
murders. She cleans the parts of the night he doesn't see
and the sun before he knows it.

Instead of saying "I love you" every day—because he flinches
she teaches him to clean, to bleach, to scour.
This is her language, and as her body grows more tired,
those gnarled fingers—each one wearing championship rings
of swollen joints and paper skin—grow weaker,
she cleans, bleaches, and scours less.

II. Brown Dad

Flexing his free hand, Brown Dad stood in the doorway.
"The water's too hot. It hurts my hands," he said,
before flinging the mug across the room.
It shattered in the sink, his aim always good.

After Monster picked up the pieces
and washed the dishes,
his father said, "thank you." "—"
Brown Dad's eyes bugged out, irises shrinking
till they were black islands in a sea of white,
and he repeated a lesson he'd learned:
"When someone thanks you, what do you say?"
"You're welcome."

III. White Mom

                        Her hands swell from exhausted dehydration,
              not like White Grandma's because that kind of work:
                    housekeeping, cotton picking, and canning
                          is a long time ago but still haunting.

Monster catches glances of her haunted hands when she warms
Nutrisystem, shakes Slim Fast, or juggles a microwaved potato,
but only in the few minutes between coming home from work
              and going into her office to work on her resume.
         Two years from retirement, she'll take another job
                            an hour farther away.

                    "I need the money," she says, but means
White Family needs the money and Brown Dad's hands hurt.
                    "I need the money," she says, but means
                I sure as shit ain't gonna clean houses.

Using Chinatown to Converse with Brown Dad

For me, Chinatown is lunch specials with Jackie Chan
on the wall, one bag of cheap taro, another of mung bean
desserts, a samurai sword, and four baby turtles named
Leonardo, Donatello, Mike, and Raph (I like naming in sets).

The purchases perform Asian from a country, a continent,
and half a race away in an attempt to find home.

For Brown Dad, Chinatown is a copycat visit,
one bag of hand exercisers, another of fidget spinners,
a still-headed roast duck, a staring grilled fish,
and three adult turtles with no names but long claws.

The purchases perform paternity without planning
in an attempt to make a home.

Home is a tiny aquarium with seven turtles cramped together–
four babies and three adults–taking turns breathing.

Suffering is a love language that has crossed
an ocean and culture, poverty and wealth.

Know this: *I love you and want you happy.*
What you want, though, doesn't matter.

Miracle Meat

Meat was our communion,
and during the desperate times,
White Mom was our priest.
She would cook when Brown Dad felt shame
from a meatless kitchen as if a bowl full of only
beans and rice said something about masculinity.
He was like a Catholic who cut out
before the end of mass and stockpiled
so much guilt he had to accept the body
to break even, if for only a week. Never mind how
a wafer could settle a stomach or wine soothe an ache.

Hours before dinner, she'd be in the cabinets
searching for the dustiest, dented-
and-unlabeled cans. It all went in the pot.
She called it goulash, and we ate it
with Brown Dad looking on, the fear of Filipino
hunger threatening starvation for uncleared plates.

At the bottom of every serving,
like a surprise birthday party, was a cube of meat.
On seeing it, our faces disappeared,
and you'd only see four bowl-cut halos.

Years later, tired of beans, rice, ramen, I asked White Mom,
how did she transubstantiate canned corn and peas
into that miraculous meat. She said, "I used what we had,
and your father kept flats of Skippy dog food in the garage.
It's no miracle, it's desperation."

Addition by Subtraction

For White Mom, fishing was the call:
Jesus wanted fishers of men,
and her boys were learning.

For Brown Dad, fishing was an act:
it filled replaced words with movement,
occupying hands and mouths.

Both Brown Dad and White Mom knew
there was little holding us together.
If fishing would stick, it was enough.

So when I saw the roadside trout farm,
they were happy to rent a couple poles
with our next-meal money.

As they helped my brothers and me cast and reel,
even though our muscle memories could lecture,
they said, *Don't catch anything*.

We can't afford it. We spent an hour fighting fish
and skills. For us, fishing at a trout farm wasn't
about catching, it was about losing.

There Is a Call If You Can Hear It
after "untitled" by Mariflor Ramos

We are solemn when the artist describes inspiration:
her family eating lunch between rows and rows of grape vines.
They sit on the ground because not enough has been picked,
and boxes only make good chairs if they are full or empty,

never in half-measures. As she describes it, I think of a kuya,
an uncle, telling me about the layers of clothes and the heat,
how planes dumped pesticides on the fields while he worked
just as she describes having to wear long sleeves and a sweater

while under a baking sun that feeds and fuels green bunches
that feed and fuel you. We, the audience, hear her holy story,
taking her words in like the body and the blood of sacrifice.
There's no sound in the room but breathing, more felt

than heard. We must give space in the face of shared
histories and presents. But we should not be dignified.
Yes, the fields and the grapes are filled with sacrifice
and struggle, but out there on sun-packed earth is love,

just not in the grapes; love between the growing rows,
just not in the vines; love on dirt, not growing from it;
love wears three layers in the heat, not for the landowner
or the grocery store. Yes, there is love, just not for you
who can't taste it but eat it anyway. There is love.

Chasing a Happy Memory

Sometimes Manoys would cook pork chops
during those hours when our parents were working,
but we could still hear their stories about gangs
and night stalkers and the Darker Thans outside our door.

Sometimes Manoys would cook pork chops
seasoned with Lowry's and sitting on sticky white rice.
It was magical: the salt, the fat, the grease,
when our normal was beans and rice and absence.

Sometimes Manoys would cook pork chops
as if an answer to a child's prayers for that rare
and beautiful moment when your older brother
would turn on the stove and feed you.

Gods of the Liquor Store Video Game

Eddie's Jr. Market Liquor messed up;
they bought an arcade game, just one.
Manoys saw it as a problem to solve:
playing without paying.

They spent afternoons hammering coins
and washers, adjusting width and thickness,
testing their work by slipping homemade change
into the slot, seeing which were spit back

and which were kept, tying change to fishing line,
and changing knots. They learned nickels worked best,
flatter with string, thicker without, but always flash
a real quarter when you start or the clerk will ban you

forever. Buy one loose fun-sized candy before you leave
to play four times tomorrow. They got so good at it,
White Mom and Brown Dad thought them, us, geniuses
or video game gods, hours of entertainment on a quarter,

four total, one for each of us. When they changed the game,
the slugs stopped working, and we had to find techniques
to get more quarters from Brown Dad. Nothing worked.
Machines are easier to fool than people,

especially when those quarters are earned
by sleeping during the day, working all night
surrounded by a cacophony of machinery and meat
from the dog food factory's boiler room.

When quarters cost you the ability to hear,
you can give no more than four,
even to gods and geniuses,
before you stop hearing requests.

Like Tanked Sharks, We Circle and Bump

While some families kept the good chair for the man of the house, others saved the white meat, the fattest chop, the choicest cut, we kept the *PennySaver* every week. We'd place it on the counter next to the stack of bills and notices that repeated more than monthly.

Most often, Brown Dad would throw it away unread, too tired from consecutive graveyard shifts and side gigs, but there were one or two days a month where he would spread out those soft newsprint pages, wear his reading glasses, and scan

each category for free stuff. He'd start at the pets, then go to his interests: auto and anything garage before a begrudging scan of things he'd have to pay for. He'd call and haggle, even on free pets, asking for food and kennels on top of the unwanted.

Then we'd make the rounds, the grey booklet folded longways started to tear and blotch from handling and heavy-handed *Sharpie*. If it was furniture, he'd bring Manoys, if it were car parts or a new needless pet, he'd bring us all and say not to tell

White Mom, who'd know by the noise and shit of matted-haired dogs, wounded cats, no-longer-tea-cupped pigs, hissing turtles, aggravated iguanas, never-shutting up cockatiels and canaries, and untouchable snakes. He'd add them all to our cobbled family,

scour the next week's *PennySaver* for mates to couple animals just shades and days above abandoned. He'd have dreams of breeding and selling exponentially undesirable pets and more days off. The man who worked his job to maximize pay—graveyard bumps,

daily overtime, weekend per diems, with racking-up certifications and salary steps—also hunted for streams of income like a shark in a tank, circle and bump, circle and bump, circle and bump, taught us two things: There is a joy in fruitless plans and even the most meticulous is making this shit up.

The Genetic Memory of a Hawk

The bird of prey swooped down, arcing with the grace that comes with genetic memory, telling you to fear but live in defiance of gravity. At the bottom of the raptor's descent, it stretched its wings to slow and pulled its claws forward, dipping its talons into the meat of my cockatiel who flapped her wings against the sides of the cage, trying to leverage captivity for compromised freedom. It was quick and easy, like sinking your hand in water heated to 98° and only knowing where you end by sight. The hawk flaps its wings against the cage, trying to leverage resistance for supper, but I don't know if this swoop and this struggle are for survival or for fun. Maybe my need for reason is just genetic memory telling me to fear but live in death, or maybe my reasoning is that graceful motion where I ride pull and inertia to sink my senses into something I view as a little less than real.

Give Me a Dumb Dog

one that can't do any tricks.
The smart ones need attention,
distraction, love—the gaps a dog
fills. No, give me a dumb-as-shit
dog, always happy to see me
even in the face of abuse, one
that can be locked outside but is
still smart enough to find a way
to slink in and give the least
deserving love.

There Are Rules

Brown Dad learned the rules
with a new name tag,
the one his coworker stitched
to his oil-stained coveralls: *gook*.

He learned the rules when jobs
had no papers, work earned
cash-filled envelopes—
never a check and always short.
And his degrees didn't count
because a Filipino A equals
an American C.

He learned to sew small stars
and stripes onto his uniforms
because you can't spell America
with *chink*. He kept stacks of flags
in his locker, in his car, bought
handfuls of America at swap-meets.

He learned he could get along with
Flip grit and mother wit like a dog
facing an open field with the will to run
but for the leash.

He taught Manoy how loose leashes
are earned by having his hand up
or out first, by answering
the questions, by wearing
America in the heart.

He taught Manoy how, with slack,
he could talk story about home.
"Stop," he said, "when they hear."

Like a tagged and collared dog eyeing
free fields, moments before the pull,
Brown Dad taught Manoy how to become
all skin and no face, and how to feel
comfortable with callouses around his neck.

Part 2:
HOW TO MAKE AN ASIAN AMERICAN

Letter 2 by White Aunt

27 May, 1972
Dear Mom,

I'm sorry for leaving like this
don't' worry
I'll
        be
                back
in due time.
I just got to get away
think things over that I have done.
I can't decide which way of life is right,
My way
        or yours.
                Love
                      Always

                P.S. Don't try to find me cause you won't.
                            Don't ask sister.
                  she don't know anything about this.
                      it would only upset her more.

Buried Family History

We can't bury it like a body
in the backyard or box it in the attic
under decades of dirt, dust, and cobwebs,
but we should; instead, the brown bodies

of uncles and aunts shout it when strolling
into every room, filling every space
with sweatshop-owner confidence.
Pride seeps through their skin

from employing the kids of desperation
and never paying enough.
Instead, White Grandma's crooked hands
sign it in slow broken gestures learned from

cutting cotton, the kitchens, the canneries,
years and years of cleaning, to raise her children
to do the same; instead, Monster's skin whispers
it in all antonyms to every passerby who sees

his face and thinks: *ethnic*, but his skin is more
red than brown, not from Filipino lineage--
an indelible colonizer footprint--
but from his redneck family

who burn in the sun but endure.

Clarinet Shrieks Raise the Dead

White Grandma rested from cleaning your rooms
and listened to Monster practice the clarinet.

She'd stop him and say, *White Aunt could play better*
and *Your White Mama would try so hard*

and *Your White Mama would cry so hard.*
He'd listen and lick his chapped bottom lip,

hungry for stories about the White Aunt who
ran away from uprooted and angry Southerners

and a home where love had a color. He hungered
for those moments when White Grandma stopped

hearing the instrument's shriek and disappeared
while White Aunt stood near promising

never-conversations, a Mixed Cousin in her belly,
tennis shoes tied and ready to go.

Mixed-Race Tax

When Brown Friend comes over, I tap on the top 40 playlist,
avoiding the mixed-race tax I have to pay to share my latest
and greatest macro- and microaggressions as if dehumanization,

intended and subtle, can make year-end lists or be whittled down
into a yelp-like review of a trendy restaurant. If I play my music,
at a heartfelt moment a singer will twang loss that shares little

with our petering out prospects and promotion pass overs
or reading rooms to find our face, you know, the mini attacks
on our melanin-heavy hearts; country-broke still wears wealth

of skin, after all. Brown Friend says, "The singer lost me at
gonna get me some," meaning success and breaking language
are twins in the hands that are never ours and rarely colored.

I don't tell him I heard this music in the womb.
This is my bottle of formula when breast milk went bad.
White Mom fed me with her voice and sang and suffered

and sang and persisted and sang alone.
Sometimes I turn up the volume because we forget,
in the comfort of the choir, to admire the solo.

Sometimes I turn it down because we forget,
while admiring the solo,
the comfort of the choir.

Every Other Word Is Silence: A Broken Pantoum

If white is the absence color,
I'm half brown
and half nothing
build an identity with this

I'm half brown,
just enough to be passed over
      for that date
      a job
      some happiness
build an identity with this
with the absence of love, stability, and joy

just brown enough to be passed over
      for that date
      a job
      some happiness
filled with aspiration to pick up these piece and build
with the absence of love, stability, and joy
create a vocabulary where every other word is silence

filled with aspiration to pick up these piece and build
and half nothing
create a vocabulary where every other word is silence
if white is the absence of color

White Not-Cousin in Tennessee Reads Her Ancestry

"I'm part Black!"
Her glee is almost muted
amongst her collection
of Mammy cookie jars,
constant macro-aggressions,
and White Jesuses.

Black blood means
proximity to pain.
She feels forgiveness
catch fire through her veins,
that rush of salvation
through scarification,
like her fourth baptism.

Oh the joy,
oh the pride,
all the while she ignores
that but for the one Black ancestor,
there are generations
before and after holding the keys.

Her ancestry results is
a smooth piece of leather,
soft from use,
but only on one end.

Holidays Are Hurricanes

and the winds and floods are coming. You could prepare
the house with boards and taped Xs on the windows,
but the water keeps rising when White Uncle enters.

The n-words sprinkles like rain, the hate in sheets.
It smothers the mouths of his half-Mexican kids,
chokes his half-Black grandsons until they evolve gills.

When you offer him rice, he says,
"you and Junior got them chinky eyes
'cause your pregnant moms ate chow mein."

When he finds the nutcracker, he asks grandson,
"what's missing?" And the smiling kid,
who lives in the flood shouts, "n------- toes!"

And you pray for the rain to stop,
for the water to recede,
and for sins to be cleansed.

We Internalize It Young

When I took my half-Asian nieces to Chinatown—
their first time—they started making kung fu noises
for the whole 45-minute slow-freeway drive.
A block from the restaurant, Nani says,
"Okay, get the racism out of your system."
And they filled the car with ching-chong gibberish
in their little munchkin voices like the latest
chipmunk single by a white supremist band.
In the absence of modeled Bruce Lee battles,
they avoid fake punches and jabber away
with excessive bows and squint their
naturally squinted eyes. Racism never sounded
so cute and, oddly, never felt so sad.

The Reason for the Shirk

I called Brown Brothers *Manoys*
without knowing what it meant
or why they deserved it, but I knew
it had *because-I-told-you-so* power.

I grew up having to call them *elder*
because it was custom, a holdover of a life
that Brown Dad tried to shirk daily,
that Manoys had to shirk from their tongues,
that I had to shirk before it was mine.

I had to call them *manoy* when I caused
the shirk. For them, I was an anchor baby
was a promised drowning, a White thing
that needed no title.

When I grew under the weight of *manoy*
and what it meant to them, I shirked it
like I was trained to. But in that move,
I cut off the tip of my own tongue,

that last sweet receptor that let me know
what home could taste like. I'm left
with phantom flavors, and the language
in my mouth tastes salty like the ocean,
metallic like force, bitter like oppression.

Monster Imagines the Surgery

Monster replaces his skin, loses the confusing shade
of iron-rich dirt that says he could be anything but White
and replaces it with a Hot Topic pale. His skin feels far away,
like his flesh floats near it, not touching, but now more his.

He exchanges his nose, too, shaving its blunt and bulbous shape
down to sharp angles. His fingertips no longer fit in the nostrils;
picking a winner is harder, but he feels nothing is lost.

Monster returns to poetry readings, the ones where he felt
out of place: too dark in a White room, not dark enough
in Brown and Black rooms, and always performing.
When Monster speaks, though, in either room, when Monster
describes his experience living Mixed,
his voice seems to ring empty.

Before, light would reflect on his Brown skin
and project out onto the world, shading and tinting
everything in hues of color. Now the light, reflected
on his White, White skin, makes the world too stark,
too acute, all edges sharp enough to cut.

Monster returns home with his new skin and face
and in every white-lit room he is always seen.

I Stopped Drawing Because of a White Girl

Once, I showed my sketchbook to a girl,
the pages filled with my fascination
for eyelids that had that crease. You know,
the one that makes an Asian eye not,
the one that carries the happiness,
the hate, the rage, and the age.

The book's leaves, burnt at the edges,
captured eyes unlike mine and oh the noses,
half the proportions, angular, refined.
I showed my sketchbook to a girl
because I didn't have the words to tell her

I liked her, and she saw all the White eyelids,
the White noses, many of them hers.
I showed my sketchbook to a girl,
and she wordlessly gave it back,
wordlessly refused me seeing her
as only pieces of a whole,
wordlessly refused me—hating me.

How to Clean Unhealing Wounds

White Grandma fills our house and her mobile home
with synonyms, with the rhythmic swish and click
of a mop across the floor, with her voice—like a scratched
country record—saying you can't help because you do it wrong.
But she'll show you again, with all the lifehacks she's learned,
not to cut corners, no, but to make things microscopically
easier for some unimaginable later.

The slosh of water in a bucket and the creak of a wringed rag
are sounds of her search for a dead Mama, the one who was
so young and left all them kids to a no-good alcoholic;
for a dead Daddy, the one that took her in, loved her
with quiet and constant calm, adoption, and her first shoes;
for her daughter, the one that was born with the last good genes
in her blood, the one that has been gone, gone, gone,
without a word.

White Grandma fills her cleaning bucket by putting pain
in the solution to wash everything leading up to the doorway.
You can watch, but you can't help.

The Calculus of Help and Hope

White Uncle hides pieces of salvation,
like Voldemort's horcruxes, in handiwork,
in the jobs he does for other people.

He tallies a list in his head like calculating
the difference between the price per pound
of a brand on sale versus the generic

when the tag lists the former in ounces
and the latter in some other metric
you should know but know it's not the same.

If you ask him what he has done for salvation,
the answer is always in the present tense
as if the ledger trailing behind was cleared

by declaring bankruptcy. You know about
stealing from his mother and painting Kay's
house, about the dudes he'd shack with

for money and smack before some of us
could normalize bisexuality and building
Lucius' fence. You know because you saw

White Grandma cry and his paint-stained
shorts you bought him from Costco. You
know because you saw him hug a man tight

when he hopped on the back of Red's bike
and your borrowed drill in his hand peak
over wooden slats next door. Each screw

burrowing into the wood made him a pirate
burying flecks of treasure. The tip of this
nail holds this sin. The point of that one

holds that crime. Like a wizard or a teen
with a magic kit, he hopes patching
a mobile-home park without pay

manages your attention away from
some sins he committed and others
that need no forgiveness.

The Emotionally Orphaned Search for Traditions

White Mom mythologizes every Thanksgiving-day gesture,
declaring "we will do *this* every year," picking up her phone
to make a note but getting distracted by a notification and
never touching its screen.

This means caramelized crust on a socially-distanced Korean grill
        during the pandemic.
This meant separate trays from different stops at a Universal Studios
        food court.
This meant all the family, windows steamed from human humidity,
        lap plates and spills.
This means a sad table, a setting for two, and the memory of plates
        with nothing on them.

White Mom uses her father's decayed green thumb
to plant heritage seeds that never take.
She changes White Elephants,
starts and ends bracelets half-charmed,

gifts collectibles from clearance bins.
She leaps from belief to belief, going all in,
like a sucker, on inside straights of angels
and astrologies to fill in sister-shaped gaps.

I am with her, hungry for a fitting form.
I map my own absences in natal charts,
record my ancestry through planetary rulers,
download the apps, calendar Mercury in retrograde,

pray to explain away fist-sized holes
and frustrating Zoom drops, but Monster
refuses the horoscopes about me,
rejecting the idea that paths are marked and typed.

I have learned what White Mom could not:
the gaps are in our bodies, fully realized signs
are synonymous with labels,
and half a leap is really just a stumble.

Like a burlap bag of possum babies

Inside, the three of them know
what's coming next won't be good.
It's more the tension of not knowing
than the rough drag across the forest floor.
You can put two and two together:
burlap sack + living creatures
equals a drowning.

Don't worry, this is only abandoning.

I hear their distinct yelps
as the sack slams and sticks to a fallen tree,
rounds over the top,
then drops off.

These memories are too much of me,
        but I hope,
                I want
                        death.

When I've chosen the spot,
I tip the bag over. They tumble.
I take one last look at each,
measuring the shape of their
future and hoped-for absence.

There's the time I told Mixed Sister
I hated her partner, together they were
subtraction by addition. The memory
was round, bulky, and fuzzy,
like the biggest prize at a carnival
but cared for, uncovered
by sun damage and dust.

There's the last time I had sex with White
Girlfriend. We had already broken up. I think
she was hoping one last time would turn it.
The memory was sleek and dingey
like a cat no one wants that slides
into a room, all unearned confidence.

The last memory clung to the bag bottom,
it's sharp claws piercing my fingertips.
The little monster was the least fleshed:
fangs and claws and oh so many arms
that could catch and hold pieces of me.
It was the night Brown Dad heard me read,
the night he said I was an embarrassment
and he wished all the years I have worked
never happened.

If I were a proud parent of these parasites,
I'd say something, but brokenness keeps
me quiet and tearless. I walk away,
hearing the woods echo
while Brown Dad's ghost
      gnashes,
           slashes,
                  and follows.

I know it's behind me,
reaching out
its claws sinking into my back,
    soft,
        smooth
            like dipping a toe
                into warm water.
Even now, I can feel it slither deeper
into my center to catch my fingertips
and seep into this poem.

While Brown Dad wishes
I never learned to write,
he makes sure he shapes
and forms my limits.

Part 3:
MIGRATION MEANS ALWAYS BEING HAUNTED, AND RETURNING MEANS GIVING GHOSTS SUBSTANCE

Letter 3 by White Aunt

Date Unknown
Dear Mom,

You don't have to worry about me
I have got a roof over my head
I'm eating well.
I left for me.
I was pregnant by Greg.
    But I had a miscarriage the night I went to the doctor.

Don't worry about looking for me.
I won't come home.
no one knows where I'm at.

Did daddy ever shoot that black n----- Thompson?
I changed my viewpoint about black men.
Greg he told me he didn't care
    I was pregnant.
        The next boy I go with will be white.

The best of wishes now.
I'll try to write again.
hope all your holidays will be nice.
Remember I'll always love you.

The New Rules

Fifteen years living only at night,
running from daylight sounds and hours,
Brown Dad crawled out of the third world
and the ghetto with a pair of kids
from each struggle. As soon as we moved
into our suburban home, he bought chickens
to make us aware of danger, to make us
eggs for breakfast, to make us feel at home.

The chickens angered the White neighbors,
as did the '78 Mustang, the '83 Cadillac,
the '92 Jetta killing everything in the front
from oil saturated grass to his hopes,
wants, and attempts at fixing them.

From his eyes, he saw a backyard menagerie,
a mansion to live in, and a stable of cars,
but he also saw the neighborhood's families
grow, the neighborhood's kids become friends,
become families while his drove cities away
to find normal. His accomplishments felt like
blemishes on the pure and clean neighborhood.

Evergreen Bowling Lanes

Construction paper cutouts
of red, orange, yellow leaves
taped to the wall, signaling Fall
in ways California's trees don't.

The walls are painted with tiki images
and large green bamboo, all decked out
as paradise in a bowling alley.
The competition was glossy and LCDs.

Here, it was projectors and handwriting,
some paint, and schizophrenic paradises:
mid-90s paradise rockabilly,
late-90s paradise streaked with red,

celebrating laser tag next door,
but always underneath and returning:
grass huts, hula girls, and surfers.
Here is a struggle to be identified,

different from your expectations,
a declaration: "You cannot know
me from how I look." The competition,
clean and automated, always wins.

The bulldozers come, pushing, crunching,
breaking the evergreen paint underneath.
They don't have to know you
to destroy you.

Movie Theater Summer Camp

We ran up and down the aisles,
sat in the front and the back row,
hopped movies after the previews,
saw Tim Burton's *Batman* six times
on those hazy days when you need
the kids to shut up and be safe.

Brown Dad had twelve hours to eat
breakfast/dinner, sleep, and watch
Monster and White Brother, sparing
a minute to curse the farmer's lobby
and teachers' unions for their resistance
to year-round school, so he treated
his White kids to cinematic adventures.
But there were rules:

Watch whatever. Sit wherever. Don't ask
for money. Don't you dare wake him
till the movie has played twice.

Filipinx Crab Mentality

The water, just past my feet, is cold here.
Even this close, I can feel it choke my pores closed.
The sand is packed hard and thick, crushed
by slow geographic ages rather than crumbled
and spit in the violence of ash and monsoons.
I am the crab who has moved boulders from divots
to make a home. I am the crab who picks at
carcasses the ocean drops at my doorstep.
I am the crab who runs from the approaching tide,
and the one who hunkers down when it catches me.

My DNA remembers water as warm as blood
that could open my pores and limbs in acceptance.
My ancestral feet remember sand lightly coating toes
like sugar on a donut but sometimes brown,
sometimes black. I was the crab you find
in a floating clump of seaweed and the solitary one
you caught in your net beneath all the fish,
feeding off the dead and the sick sinking to the bottom.
I am the one crab you hunt in the rocks,
quick to scurry, but my claws are ready,
for I have seen seas and sand and know the tide
is always coming. You are always coming.

Word Problems

> *Not merely a passageway to knowledge, language is a form of knowing by itself; a people's way of thinking and feeling is revealed through its music*
>
> — *Haunani-Kay Trask*

Seeing the world through mixed-race eyes
and expressing it with one tongue, I tell
myself, "there is more to culture than language."

But I know wrong feels like a word problem
for distance without velocity. I speak Brown Dad's
Crab Talk by grabbing at the legs above and kicking
the heads below, but language is the context needed

for knowing why. Layer one-tined tongues in the mouths
of Filipinx ancestors and their stories filled with soil
multiplied by colonization, and the product is negative.
There is a ton of remainder because the formula is wrong.

With only one tongue, half of me is missing
and if I saw the words of me, I wouldn't recognize
the shape, the content, the meaning, or the solution.

If you ask if I speak Tagalog

in my head I'll call you racist,
but aloud I'll say no. No, but
my family spoke Cebuano.
No, but my older brothers did
until their accents held them
      three
           grades
                  back.

No, but Brown Dad outlawed it.
No, but I'm sorry that I don't.
No, but it's like an amputation.
No, but it never heals.
No, because
      you ask
           and ask
                and ask.

When the Invasive Becomes Domestic
After Irene Suico Soriano

So starved of home on my tongue,
I'm reading a poem about the death
of Filipina domestic workers who will
be buried in foreign soil, and I perk up
at the words Cebu and Cebuano and say
other Filipino phrases out loud, hoping
my mouth finds them familiar one day.

I knew the anxiety of metal-to-metal tapping
on room number plates with housekeeping keys
before entering the unknown. First, I knew to
use a towel to prop the door open for plausible
deniability if something goes missing or
so passersby can hear me call. Second,
I knew no matter the situation, say sorry

if the occupant is in the room. Third,
I knew to go about my business, pretend
the occupant isn't there, but listen for
their words, listen for their movements.
Fourth, coil exhausted muscles just in case,
but I never reminded myself: I am a man,
and I never thought about these Brown Aunties

and what it meant for them to go
tap,
        tap,
                tapping
on occupied doors and the messes
they were expected to clean.
I never knew to listen for an Aunty's call
and wouldn't know the Cebuano word
for help if I heard it.

The Desert Tortoise Is New

but over 50. We name him *Manoy Honu*,
a mixture of tongues, ours but not.
Manoy: Cebuano for elder, like elder brother.
Honu: Hawaiian for turtle, like sea turtle.
Both words willfully wrong, as if we're joking
on ourselves, as if *Manoy* was named by a child
still learning the language and these are the only
words the child has confidence in.

We name him *Manoy*, the only Cebuano word
I remember, the only one I was taught,
the only one I have forgotten, because my Eastern
Brown Brothers used it, hid behind it for authority,
because my Western mind refused and refuses
Brown Authority, refused and refuses honorifics.

The word is from such a distant and never me,
I don't pronounce it correctly, never correctly.
My White Mom's Southern drawl slows my speech,
and I elongate the first syllable: *Mah,* like mother.

We name him *Manoy* to show him respect, to remember
on the journey to now we've held tight to some things
that didn't matter and let slip the sacred.

The stories are in the gaps and the silences

like when your grams and elders, the Brown ones,
talk story about when Uncle did that crazy thing
that was so Uncle, about the party when Aunty
got drunk, said that thing, and everyone cried
because it was mean and true and truly mean,
about how the kids were all gathered together,
blurring the lines between sibling and cousin
and friend, and how relational titles served
nothing other than White-Western confusion.

The stories are in the gaps and the silences,
the moments that come just after the story is shared,
just before the next one is told, when you realize
Aunty in the story isn't Aunty sitting with you.
When did Aunty's drinking stop and why?
When did the kids stop gathering and why?
When did Uncle stop being so Uncle?
The stories are in the gaps that hint
at the hard lines we draw, the never-agains

and *we-mean-its*. The stories are in the silences
we pay to honor what we're losing if we didn't
change. The best stories, the ones we can truly
learn from, are the ones our grams and elders
cannot speak because the silence is the only thing
holding back the threat.

Bury It When You Land

White Mom dislikes talk about migration.
When she tries, she punctuates with hopeful
doom scrolling her work email.
She tells me about coming to California,
about a working 13-year-old slapping
sandwich layers together during lunch rush,
about a secret account and hidden cash
in books, about saving for private school
just to distance from them,
her voice lowers: Blacks.

                Brown Dad dislikes talk about migration.
                When he tries, he punctuates it in sudden
                departures for car repair and swap meets.
                He tells me about entering White countries
                about working weeks for free to show his
                ability only to be paid under the table.
                About "Sure," he'd say. "Pay what you can,
                when you can." About how he could count
                "what he could earn," but was silent
                "when they didn't pay."

The story I want to hear, though,
the one I press and ply her with drinks for,
is the why: Why move here?

                The story I want to hear, though,
                the one he tells indirectly in chores,
                is the why: Why migrate?

The story I want to hear—the one I rewrite
and revise questions to dig with like
useslessly sharpened shovel blades—
is the story of a fracturing family
hoping a continental shift would somehow
make them whole.

                The story I want to hear—the one I ask
                only in my head because all tongues
                to him are cutting blades--
                is the story of a man moving oceans away
                with a family on his back, keeping them together
                but not whole.

The story I want to hear,
the one she can't tell because
there is no direct White translation
for the words is how:
"We were wrong."

                                      The story I want to hear,
                                        the one he can't tell because
                          like any muscle, the tongue needs exercise,
                          and his doesn't move is how: "I had enough
                                                strength to carry only us."

This Year We'll Try Color

The young and the nerds use back-to-school sales as new year's resolutions, between each item on the shopping list, read: *this time will be different* and check off the supplies in your cart, the color-coded tabs and folders that make recognition easy and quick and will prevent the loss of essays and math problems; never mind the *Bango Tags* your imported ancestors carried to prove their identity on pay day and their worth for credit; never mind, like the styles single-subject notebooks, the metal and shape were chosen to distinguish the differences between Asian and Pacific Islander skins that untrained eyes could not see; never mind the plantation owners paying for just bodies to cut the cane but used a color-coded system to pay lighter skinned ones a bit more as if degreed burns under the sun deserve degreed rewards; never mind losing a hexagonal tag meant you were no longer a Japanese worker, Losing a numbered, brass tag meant you were no longer a Filipino worker, losing a tin circle meant you were no longer a Chinese worker, you were just Japanese, Filipino, Chinese and worth nothing without that color-coded tab; never mind that that is not you, that that was not your father or uncles; just focus on how, this year, you're going to try a new highlighter: pink for main ideas, yellow for support, and a box of *Bic* black pens for everything else.

When Trapped

From my parents, both White and Brown,
I inherited the ability and want to leave.

Brown Dad, when trapped, would storm
and threaten about disappearing, about escaping.
"You will starve, and I will not care."

White Mom, when trapped, would find small escapes
like forgetting a power cord, calling on her office phone,
forgetting an email, each more ridiculous than the last.

Both of them have itchy feet and dart their eyes like a cop,
clearing the room for exits before they can enter.
This is my inheritance: feeling trapped, even in comfort.

When trapped, I test every lock and latch, lay ambushes
for you--small, skipped details—creating reason
for you to push me away.

The Travel Tax

Traveling costs, with every descent
into someplace new, pain.

Pain, like a blade sliding through skin,
skates from the bridge of my nose down through my cheek.

Pain, just below the skin, forces one slow,
hard tear at a time.

Pain is a current flowing under slow tears,
up my brow before falling down to the sides of my mouth.

One tear at a time rolls, as I snap my jaw shut.
My teeth begin to throb.

Pain separates me from my face.
Pain reminds: For my parents,

going from one place to another isn't traveling,
it is needing, it is fleeing, it is surviving.

Filling Cebu with My Last Breath

White Mom said, "It's not safe there," and she knows.
She got me vaccines and visas, pictures and passports.
I nodded, inhaled, felt the restraint around my waist
before wheels up and saw my organs liquefying and seeping
through ears and tear ducts.

White Mom said, "They're kidnapping Americans."
Like a priest blessing bread, she handed me my passport.
"Take this," she said. "Protect it. It is all of you."
And when I got into the back of Brown Uncle's car,
I inhaled and imagined swearing my family had no money

and wondered if my parents would pay the ransom no matter
how low. "It's not safe there," White Mom said, and she knows.
When Light-Skinned Aunty unpacked my bag and asked
for my passport: "I'll put it in our safe." I wanted to say no,

imagining she'd sell it to identity thieves to take all of me.
I inhaled and remembered Brown Dad belting Manoys,
and between thwaps swearing they'd starve but for America.
The one time I went to Cebu was filled with last breaths
because White Mom had never been, and Brown Dad was
haunted.

The Rot Is on the Inside

For a week, I chased Light-Skinned Cousin—the one who quit
school, moved home to help run the business, and floundered.

Catching him after he "slept one off" and slurped down SPAM,
eggs with a beer chaser, we drove around Cebu,
and I measured time by passing the flattening renovation scaffolds
and folding white-and-cream splattered tarps around
the University of San Carlos.

Its facade bright and light in the midday. "Oldest college in Cebu,"
he'd say every other pass. His caramel hair held volume, even with
the windows down, sweat covered skin that burned too easily and
confirmed the legacy of colonizers. "Your father got his degree
here. Mine, too."

Once, we went inside where the paint was browning and chipped,
thick from coverups. The building smelled like old and cracked
dirt freshly turned, like desperate and stagnate death.

We ended the days with the usual: I'd ask if he was coming
to dinner. He'd say no. I'd give him money, just enough to get
through the night.

While My Veins Thicken, While My Heart Pounds

We've been eating the body and drinking the blood since 1521,
when the Spanish downsized the holy by laying off
elemental and divine middle management and outsourcing
customer service to priests, tithes, and confessionals.

I've been eating the body and drinking the blood since birth,
when Brown Dad took over for John Smith and his golden plates
and said there shall be no other books but the good book
while he refused to enter a church or to kneel.

Spain has been eating the body and drinking the soda since 2021,
when the Philippines opened new markets with its first *Jolliebee*
to sell its sweet spaghetti and *Chickenjoy* in an attempt
at reciprocity that mostly goes in one direction.

I've been eating the body and drinking the soda since 1996,
when I visited home for the first time and bought the combo:
hotdog and noodles with fried chicken. On my first slurp,
on my first crunch, my tastebuds knew the salt and the sweet

as if they had been laid on my tongue and blessed by the divine.
With every bite, I imagine John Smith and his blonde hair
being ground and torn by my teeth until he no longer exists.
With every bite, I feel I am earning an identity that was stolen.

My Place in Kingsport, Tennessee

At the *Shoney's* table, surround by cross-country relatives
I've never met before. We are related by obligation
to the dead and aging but not by blood.

White Uncle turns to me, tuning out the women
and what he'd call cackling: *She tried to take
her daddy's gun the other day,* he says

with a chunk of chuckle and dash of disbelief.
*She don't know, her and our daughters,
hen-pecking in business ain't theirs.*

I nod because I know it's White Uncle's
father-in-law losing memory. It's also
White Uncle's country, and I know

where he expects my place to be.
It's also White Uncle's table, and I know
we will tussle over the coming bill

as a sign of who's got the bigger paycheck,
and I know I will let him win.
She don't know you can't take a man's

whole gun, he says, *so I filed the pin
and gave it back* and let him feel
dangerous and protected.

No matter if he can't
discern the difference.

That Soothing Warmth and The Pressure

An identity is questioned only when it's menaced.

—James Baldwin

White Co-worker rests her hand on my mixed-race
shoulder in that paternalistic way, like guiding
a half-ton bull by a slack harness. "Don't speak
for White people," she says when I describe
how my Tennessee is different from hers
or when I agree with our rhythmless coworker
about a shared genetic inability to find the beat,
despite him running the world, despite my skin.

Or she rests her hand on my forearm in that motherly way,
like the knowledge of a gun is enough for a mugging.
"I am White, and I feel triggered," she says jokingly
when I say America celebrates Grandparents Day
in nursing homes or when I joke about how
the community gardener cannot hand shovels
to minoritized visitors and ask them to turn soil.

I didn't say *White gardener* because I felt the hand
rest on my throat, in that White way, like napping
at the beach while someone piles handfuls of sand
on your body and you wake up feeling that all-around
warmth, begging you to return to sleep, and the pressure.

Made in the Image

We are as perfect as the creator's ability to translate
the inspired nothing into something, like a sculptor
chipping away at marble made of planets and galaxies,
trying to find the essence of something in the vastness of not.

And we are, like that artist, frantically wheeling out
the unused pieces in the alchemy of birth,
filling a wheelbarrow with rubbish and faith
in a vision of something under the layers.

But we are as perfect as our creator's aphasia
to describe the nothing, which means, like God,
we condemn what we are not and damn
anything that looks like love without dominance.

Part 4:
TOUCHING FROM A DISTANCE

Letter 4 by White Aunt

Date Unknown
Dear Mom

I'm just fine.
I'm eating right.
I got enough clothes—
very happy.
I'm on my way to Canada with a lot of people.
I can truthfully say I'm very happy.
It's hard but I'm making it.
I've lost enough weight to wear a size 12 or 10 pants.
don't need anything
just wanted you to know that I was alright
doing just fine.
Listen if Sister didn't give my presents away to my friends,
ask her to do it for me.
Tell her she can have my clothes if she can wear them.

I had a nice Christmas at here
home
       with my friends
we had a small turkey, dressing, conjell,
hot rolls, freshed cooked greens cooked Mexican style.
I also had a nice New Year's
had a big party cause we were still traveling to Canada.
We were about 300 miles away from there.

Well I'm running out of things to say.

Tell Dad I had a nice holiday
Tell the kids hi and not to worry.
Remember I love you.
I'll write when I get a chance.

You Know What You Did

It's a violent microaggression
when your White coworkers leave
the choice between a coconut donut
or a half-eaten, glazed cruller.

Selecting between sinking your teeth
through a thin layer of whiteness
and nothing is a form of guilt-ladened
consent. It is purely manufactured.

Be honest, and leave me a plain cake donut.
That tough, unflavored crust is the familiar.
And I will choke it down with tap water
so as not to give you the satisfaction.

I Presented My Writing at The Twin Towers Correctional Facility

I put it in my bio, but I never say it was for poetry.
I put it in my bio, but I never say it was for prisoners.
I put it in my bio, but I never say it was for a cause.
I put it in my bio, but omit I was invited by the guards,

for the guards to have reason to eat Hawaiian food and wear lei.
Their plate lunches stacked—rice, mac salad, teri chicken and beef—
so they can drown out my history book presentation with teeth
grinding meat under the guise of understanding one group's

disproportionate incarceration and missing the point seen
in the pictures of knee-bounced babies at a table covered
in cut flowers and string, the makings of lei for the rare graduations
and too common arrivals, or the gowned aunties and grandmas

shuffling hula at scholarship fundraisers for the young adults
who rely so much on family for identity and so, so often
reside in places like this, removed from love
by walls and bars and oceans and countries.

I put it in my bio, but I never say I cashed the speaking fee
while on the hustle, cancelling class without reporting it
so I could double dip without using sick time to help
pay down student loans that didn't match the worth of the degree.

I put it in my bio, but I never say I hated having to lean in
to hear my escort's hushed and protective instructions
or the casual attitude to two dudes at the back of the elevator,
hands cuffed,
    heads down,
        facing the back,
            pressed against the wall
                like it's normal.

Fishing in Dirty Water

Brown Dad's tacklebox was heavy.
I remember flakes of rust like iron snow
sprinkled over the lures, the knives,
the hooks, the lines, the pliers too
corroded to open, floaters cracked
like broken bulbs on a burnt sidewalk
Christmas tree. Little of it was purchased,
all of it found, scavenged, and necessary.

My tacklebox, and the contents in it,
is clean and shiny, unscratched, unused,
and unneeded. Price tags dangle.
I never bother taking them off; it's doubtful
I'll keep anything, but I keep coming
back, as if I saw something, once,
and I remember only the shape,
never the substance.

But something in the repetition of tying
a hook and weights, of making sure
the knots are right, hints at nirvana.
Jesus knew this, I think. But there is also
an anxiety, the moment before the moment,
the want to meet the need.

White Grandma called to warn me

the other day, she said: "I just wanted
to hear your voice." "Well, here it is:
Hi." She said, "Thank you" and hung up.

She was telling me: *This quarantine costs
so much. I am losing so much.*

I was telling her: *I'm here to give you
the minimum because I don't have
the vocabulary or the resources to give
you what you need, to give you more.*

She was telling me*: When you've been
abandoned by parents, have lost 1.5 children,
have broken every foundation you've built
until all you can do is rent space for an immobile
mobile home, you'll take the minimum, that* "Hi,"
and make it stretch, make it mean everything.

The Bullets That Were Close to Me

My friend has a bullet lodged in his leg.
He isn't a criminal or veteran. His came
from a hold up at work. He said,
"That year I had a lot of therapy,
but getting shot wasn't the problem."

My student tells me she can't
come to class anymore. "But
you're here now," I say. She pulls
open her jacket, revealing the bandage
wrapping her arm. "He walked up

to my mom and me. I don't want
to leave home anymore."
Another student missed his final,
but his classmates were there,
crying, crying, crying.

"Speedy's dead."

and his absence lingers
like an unfinished sentence.
I expect to see him in every class,
every semester, every school.
I'm waiting for it to finish.
It's as if living broken, for me,
is all any of us can ask.

Gatekeepers Create a Mission Statement

I enter the meeting angry. I exit the meeting angry,
and in between my colleagues say, "We must stop
systemic racism." They say it should be our mission
statement, as if this is an original declaration,
and I'm angry.

While hearing how we should break the foundation
we're built on, I'm reading the eighth draft of an essay,
two weeks after the semester is over from a Black student
who lost her cousin last week and is still
figuring out how her computer works.

We're doing it already, adopting the language of uprising,
hopping in front of the march from the safety of zoom,
preparing the way to admit those who say they down
while continuing to exclude those who are down.
I say, "We are the gatekeepers.

The best we can hope is to teach navigation and language.
The best we can hope is to model a way up and out."
They say, "No, we must be anti-racist"
while I respond to the student,
"you're still plagiarizing.

Give credit and space to the ideas you're using,
put them in quotes and cite." I quiet, knowing
these same voices are the ones who lock
the classroom door as soon as class starts,
who turn away the wrong paperwork,

who hide behind "there's nothing I can do"
but mean *I'm willing to give all of Work Me
but never Me.* While the student sends
a barely touched rewrite, my grades are late.
I know I will fail her, but I hope, I pray,

I need something different.

Death Shouldn't Be Time for Selfishness

In the room next to the dead,
it's quiet but for muted crying
and the focus on the controllable.

Did you turn off the heater?
What about dinner: the questions
that remind you to inhale.

I know that when White Grandma dies,
we will mourn her with tears
because we feel, silence because

we don't have the language,
and chores because cleaning
was all she knew. These are reminders

to inhale. But when Nani's Tutu died,
we gathered around her bed and sang.
We sang her favorite songs. We sang

with tears and with smiles. We sang
till we couldn't breathe. We sang
as the paramedics took her body.

We sang and sang and sang, and at her funeral,
we cried and danced. All the things to show
she had lived and her breath had been shared

with ours, and we live, and no reminder to inhale
was necessary. I know when White Grandma dies,
I will mourn her with tears and silence and chores

and will regret she had never been comfortable
singing. I know that when she dies,
I will need reminders to breathe.

All Brown Dad Has

is a pocket full of fidget spinners.
He gives them out to every child
he comes across, a smile on his face
that looks more like a snarl
under his mustache - or maybe
that's just how I see it. He gives
out the spinners, bought for a buck
each. What a great deal till you
buy them a hundred at a time.

He passes them out in restaurants
and stores, ignoring parental protests
to the point it feels like an assault.
It's a bit creepy, but if you know him,
Brown Dad, if you look past his kids,
past their stunted emotions, past
the distance between him and every
person he knows, you'll see a full pocket
is a pocket full of redemption spoken
in a language few can understand.

For Brown Dad, love, especially kind
and harmless love, is an assault,
and that pocket full of spinners
is everything he can crave.

Deathbed Love Languages

If I am in the room when Brown Dad dies,
his last words will be in Cebuano.
They will bubble and lilt in sound structures
that have a poetic cadence and just enough
Anglicized words, if not straight English,
to keep me putting pieces together
like an *IKEA* bookshelf without pegs.

If his siblings are in the room when he dies,
his last words will be in English.
They will create awkward syntax
to avoid problematic syllables:
Mixed Nephew's first grade teacher says
stressed vowels are long like the *a*
in *made*, but Brown Dad approaches
the short ones like crossing rickety
bridges, elongating the *a* in *b-ahhh-g*
till he is safely across and still American.

No matter who is in the room
when Brown Dad dies, he will find
a way to mix and multiply the foreign
tongues he's cultivated more religiously
than children or backyard pets
because his words of love have to be
unintelligible and unanswerable by design.

Just a Cardboard Box with a Label

At the wake--there was never a ceremony--
we passed around a Brown Uncle's ashes.

Papa told us stories of heat contracting muscles
making the body sit up while being burned.

Brown Uncle was now a white, cardboard box
and a label and some weight. No one wanted

to pay for an urn. No one wanted to live with him.
As he made his way toward me, I wondered *how*

are we supposed to hold him, like a baby or a box?
In my hands, I thought how conveniently he could be stored

and passed him on. Please, oh, please
don't let me be forgotten when I die.

House Keeping

The cleaners wipe over
the parts of middle class
I'm not comfortable with,
as I sit outside my house
like an old school father
waiting for his partner
to pop out a baby—
a duet to create the jam
but a solo when it counts.
From my seat outside,
I can hear the squeak
of rags on windows,
but made by the pressure
of activated triceps and debt.

I pace and listen to music
to drown out the reminders
of White Grandma hollering:
you people are disgusting
as she spent her one day off
between housekeeping hospitals
and worship to clean after us,
my brothers and parents.
She'd say things like: *I shouldn't
have to live like this* and
*My son, who is always
so clean, wants to take me
away from here.* We never ask
why White Uncle doesn't come,
because we know that cleanliness
and capitalism speak conflicting
languages, and it is cheaper
to keep 1,000 square feet
than to keep a person.

The Bukowskis Went Transcendental

Hank would meditate in the corner, next to the window
overlooking his overgrown garden protecting
his privacy and his pool. The chair looks like
something you'd pick up in a wrong-turn alley
you thought was a shortcut and immediately regret.

The thick upholstered chair sits low and invites
folded legs. Linda is proud of the memory; I could
see her face shine like a parent whose kid can add
without fingers. She invites the spiritual in, she says,
in all its forms. In fact, her spiritual mother is coming

today at 2pm, but Linda conflates the serenity of spirit
with the peace that comes after minoritized hands
make desperate and necessary swipes with a rag
to clean your shit for $40 an hour once a week.
Labor like that allows you to slouch towards nirvana
because you paid someone else to crawl on their knees.

White Math

A weird, scraggly vine grows between sun-bleached rocks,
its leaves are small, a little larger than mustard seeds,
the stems are dry and brittle, showing just how little water
some need to grow, showing how nature is patient
enough to let you snap limbs while paying no mind.

My White Neighbor with white hair and a white t-shirt
passes by every day, shaking his head at the dry vines
growing between the gaps of my rock garden.
From a distance, about as far away as his house,
the vines look like drying moss that bloomed after a rain

but is now reddening and browning toward death.
He mad-dogs my front yard twice a day, walking his pet
and doing White calculus: another Brown person plus
the apartment buildings filled with X number
of Brown and Black bodies equals the 7% population

needed to trigger White flight. It takes less than a month
of me living in this house before the dude
has a realtor sign posted on his lawn. I read it as:
Enough is enough, the sunbaked soil is taking back
what is owed. *Which is fine*, he thinks,

nothing can grow here anymore, anyway.

A Fulcrum Increasing Leverage and Blood

I learned early that being right pales next to staying in the room

—Claudia Rankine

Brown Neighbor talks to Black Sister, a machete in one hand
with me on the phone in the other because I'm the landlord,
the brother, the former neighbor, and a man;
she doesn't know that Black Sister's skin treats words
like light: absorbing all the hues of hate.

Racism aside, I don't want to talk to this lady,
my former neighbor, Black Sister's current one.
I didn't want to hear her honey-do lists for me
when I lived there, and I don't want to hear
her list of grievances, each one ringing racism

if you have an ear to hear: "the weeds are a fire hazard—
the ones growing in the back and the kind Black Sister
smokes—the stuff in their yard smells and attracts rats,
the property values are going down. *The property values,
Chris!*" As she talks I do math in my head:

How much do I lose by hanging up right now?
How much irritation will she bring on Black Sister?
How much under value do I charge so Black Sister
and child can get a leg up and, hopefully, stability?
Can I afford higher fences and a gardener,

an exterminator and a painter? When will I need to refinance
again, pushing back debt to save them a couple bucks?
How much to just sell? And I stay on the line,
listening to a litany of the inconsequential and the coded.

And my fingertips trace oily hash marks on the phone,
temporary math: What is the speed of a machete swing?
What are the pounds of pressure where the blade curves
near the tip, a fulcrum increasing gravity and blood?

Living in Red

The windows are shaded red
like an emergency on *Star Trek*.
The enemy is coming: be prepared.
But I know it's just my eyes.

I tint everything red in the same shades
as the red line drawn to keep me from here,
my home. On my deed, there is a covenant
prohibiting the sale to "Orientals or Blacks."

This place would not be mine if not for sacrifice
and sacrificing. I won't let myself get comfortable.
The red needs to stay, so I follow the neighborhood
social media pages, the ones with the smug pictures

of "homeless," "acting the fool," "ghettofied"
to remind me of the need to see always in red,
to remind me that people like me are not safe,
and I need to sacrifice to get them to the other side.

Part 5:
*PLEASE, OH PLEASE, BE UNTOUCHED
BY TRAUMA A LITTLE LONGER*

Dear White Aunt,

Thank you for those letters.
White Grandma kept them
and read them over and over
like a prayer to summon you
or exorcise your absence,
which is the same thing
by different means, but
I needed every tear-blurred
word, even the last one
to your friend about
the pigs that I won't
share because I want
to sculpt my memories
of you while keeping
pieces to myself,
and it doesn't matter
if they are real or true.
What matters is you
are gone to us and still
owed. I don't think
I exist without your love
for that dude Greg
or the losses you suffered
for it. I know I don't
exist without your Dad,
already itching to leave,
quitting his sullied girls
and lost boys. And I owe
that child you lost,
that mixed-race cousin
I'll never meet, for showing
your siblings love is possible
if some strings are cut first.

Dear Sherman 1

I'm sorry you feel uncomfortable around Mixed Uncle.
Like we talked about, we have to name the problem:
he's racist. There's nothing we can do about it

but love and hope and sometimes argue—at least I can.
If you feel comfortable enough, raise your voice,
call him in, remind him it's generational conquest

that gives him light skin and you dark, remind him
his kids may have come out fair, but that's genetic chance,
and the next ones might not. But I want to caution.

Don't do what I did; don't speak his language to get along.
Every word that connects scars you internally,
and you bond and you love everyone with that fair skin,

everyone but you. Don't speak his language to get along.
Every word that connects drives the conversation further
until there are no words but the ones that wound.

Dear Sherman 2

Son, I was born with a forked tongue,
missing a tine and a body without bones.
My flesh could stretch until my skin
paled and paper-thinned, could compact
until it darkened and thickened. I could
push and pull in one static gesture.

Son, my neck would have to weave into
the White women's world: the house,
the kitchen, the table, the hands always
busy, always preparing. With one hand,
I would encircle White Grandma and
White Mom with pots of lavender. I'd crush
the end of a bloom to taste its scent on my
halved tongue instead of undulating White words.

Son, at the same time, my body was outside,
standing around the grill, trading rub recipes
with White Uncle and White Cousins. I'd bring
the expensive paprika for the poorest cuts of pork
while my tongue's missing tine whispered about
Magellan's blood, dried and powdered, spilling
from the explorer's neck onto not-sovereign-for-long
soil as I would sprinkle spice on pink and fatty meat.

Son, I pray your mixed skin never loses its elasticity.
Son, may what is living in your mixed blood never dry.

Dear Sherman 3

I'm happy you like the house;
it's quiet higher up the hill.
I'm happy you have space
to hide and read and draw and play
instead of having to dance room to room
in search of unoccupied territory.

You're right, Mom and I don't argue
as much, but that's what I wanted
to talk to you about; there's a lesson.
Let me tuck you in. We got lucky,
you see. Yes, we worked hard,
but we worked hard at the right time.
Our faults were the right faults.

Look down the hill, back to that house
with a cracked floor and no foundation.
Look past the redline and remember the mice
and roaches. We weren't dirtier people there;
we're just in a different place. We just got lucky.

And Mom and I don't argue as much,
and you don't have to dance room to room
because there's so much space.
When you need to be alone, you can be
except when we dance from room to room,
music blasting through the house, screaming
at every inch, celebrating the life-lottery we've won.

It was luck, son.
Don't let the victory fool you.

Dear Sherman 4

Sorry about the name, in more ways than one.
Your mother and I bonded over the half-life we created,
a life made up of the world's races
but a country of just two and it's enough.

Sorry for having a body made for football and an eye
for strategy, but unable to play. You got those from me.
Your legs will not be hobbled, your head will not be hurt
when you are so much more than a Brown body.

Sorry for the thick glasses that feel normal. The weakened
eyesight is from both sides, and we trained you into the aesthetic
with scientists and authors decorating your walls.
Parenting is less what you are than what we hope you to be.

Sorry for all the lectures and lessons, the best-intended ones
that were always a few inches off from your context.
Hopefully you saw wisdom in them, or your mother and I are
just mad, like our parents, and that's what we never wanted.

Sorry for not being there when you needed me.
Sorry for you not being born.
Sorry for not being able to have kids.
I'm sorry, I'm sorry, I'm sorry.

It Is Barren

The garden beds in my backyard lay fallow most months
under the 260 days of Californian sun. We bought the house
partially because of them: four 5x5 beds, pregnant
as the earth and life seem to be. I till the dirt seasonally,
getting ready to plan and plant and pray. I buy seed packets
of vegetables and fruits we might actually eat, flowers
my Hawaiian wife can use to make lei, leaves for skirts,
all things practical and impermanent as if I can waste
neither time nor effort. I till the dirt seasonally, the blisters
on the pads and palms of my hands are proof of devotion,
but still, I do not tear open a single seed packet. I do not
poke a hole in the dirt or space out the spread; instead,
the planning and praying must be enough to prove
I was here and I tried.

The Village of Fathers

At the entrance, a cousin stands shirtless,
barrel-chested, a t-shirt of body hair.
He's no guard, not a good one anyway.
He nods his head as I pass. His expression
shows neither fear nor familiarity
as if anything closer were prohibited.

The archway above looks hewn from one trunk
but smooth, so smooth, from rubbing, rubbing,
rubbing the surface. And in the village proper,
silence. I see more cousins. I see brothers,
each of them sitting, staring, with children
at their feet. I can feel their eyes following,

evaluating, judging. The workmanship for each
dwelling seems to be related to the children
sitting silently: the more kids, the more skill,
the more value, the more status. I can feel each gaze
wash over me, like the moment you feel a riptide
pull you just beyond your depth. When I exit one look,

I enter another, but no expression comes with it.
I know what they see: a not-father has entered
the Village of Fathers. Childless, I have no worth
and never will. As I move deeper, surrounded by kin,
I want to leave, to run, to hide. I want to hear
the children laugh and cry. I want to hear the men

laughing and crying. I want to live in any other village
because all that is here is not me.

Manspreading Can Go So Far

I taught the student about manspreading.
You know, the posture men take
when taking more than they deserve.
I taught my student to put her bag
on the seat to the right, put her feet up
on the seat in front, rest her arm
on the seat to the left. "How is it?" I ask.
"Comfortable," she says.

The student, by the way, is a Black nerd.

Her pronouns are *she*, *her*, and *hers*,
and she got an "A" in my class,
the class she felt comfortable in,
where I taught her about power poses—
which she used daily afterward—
and to recognize how students should
be treated, how people should be treated,
how she should be treated, not an imposter
but someone deserving, demanding, expecting
a seat, maybe two or three.

And the next semester, she attended for a month
before dropping out. These small techniques
we use for comfort mean little to feeling the press
of place and the constant reminders that you are
an undeserving, unexpected, imposter,
and traitor who will never belong here.

Crafting

The wood on the desktop is worn,
covered with hobby-knife slips
and dropped-bulk divots. Mistakes
fill the absence with words, sketches,

and paint, anything to emphasize
happenstance is not consequence
and failing, failing, failing. The desk, chipped
at the edges, smells vaguely of piss on hot days

from when one of the too-many pets
hopped from floor to chair to desk
and couldn't figure out how to get back.
The desk—attempting mid-century modern

with hard edges entwining organic curves—
looks cheap and sits in our "craft room,"
the one furthest removed from the heart,
attached by an umbilical hallway. Behind me,

a trundle bed covered in cartoon sheets,
a layer of matting cat hair, and diminishing
hope. I swivel in one direction only to exit
and sit, cutting the room with a scalpel.

I leave the windows open in here to air out the place,
and it's never enough. I leave the windows open,
praying something new will enter, anything to fill
this space, but that's not physically possible.

Portrait of a Bench in New Zealand

It sits out, alone, grassy knoll around and beneath it.
The clouds are coming in but for the briefest of moments,
just enough sun to make the unfinished boards glow,
and no one is there to see it but Nani and her camera.
We are on the other side of the planet to celebrate:
ten years married, employment, no responsibilities.

She looks for these moments where absence is visible
but only to her. It's like a letter to a person
that doesn't exist, the never-future she is living,
the never-future I am living, but it's not together.

She looks for these, these moments
that look like you had just gotten up
after telling your child: *That's enough.*
Let's go home.

She looks for these,
these moments where
absence is visible.

Maybe Life Is Better When

For years, we selfishly worried about our elders,
the ones who kept their Hawaiian tongues secret
when the state dictated them cut.

There were so few in the family, we fretted
none would be there to pluck a child's name
from the world like picking flowers for lei—

a gift at a greeting—no matter
that Queen Lili'uokalani's birth name
was picked for the sore eyes her elder suffered.

As time passed, our elders did, too,
and we joked about blindly stroking
alphabetical lists of Hawaiian baby names

or going *pull Pilipino* and selecting one
based upon joyful pops across tastebuds,
words without context and removed

from meaning other than being unique
and just foreign enough for future butcherings.
Maybe our child won't have a Hawaiian name,

we consoled ourselves, *Papa didn't, and he was
the doorway to culture by blood and knowledge.
Maybe Hawaiianess isn't in a name but in the blood*

*and the heart, and maybe we don't have enough
of either to have a child, and maybe we could have
named him Kavika because that sounds so much better*

*than simply David, and I never talk
to my cousin David anyway because
he's an asshole. And maybe life is better*

*when you cut out the parts of you
you think are important, and maybe
life is better childless.*

That Old Scam

I teach Yellow Nephew to lean back in the stroller,
slouch, go non-verbal at the Disneyland gate,
allow his size to speak for him: *too young to be charged.*

It's the same scam Brown Dad ran at the drive-in:
tuck your legs under the front seat, cover the pimples
with your hand casually. And those in the trunk,

shut the fuck up or no one sees the movie.
It's the same scam we ran in the parking lot
selling driving range balls that we scooped up

to earn a little money when the movie was boring.
We'd sit in the open trunk, White Brother,
the smallest and most sickly, claimed the business.

$10 for the bucket and balls, half the price
at the range, whole price of Brown Dad's ticket.
Manoy and I kept our distance, too big for pity

too brown to be trusted. It's the same scam
that's been run on us for generations: *make yourself
diminutive and think you're winning.*

Hoping for Hanai

The Native Hawaiians had *hanai*,
an informal form of adoption
sometimes based on hope or need,
sometimes a completely open or dirty
secret, but intended to lift the family.

Running laps of capitalism and colonialism
while measuring masculinity and poverty,
I've wrecked my body by learning to hold
my piss longer than my brothers to maximize
a parent's time off and letting legs, tucked

under office desks, atrophy to earn wealth
and worth. But compulsed by culture to create life,
friends, and family, I now wish for two things:
I wish for your family structures to crumble

just enough that my house is a home for
your child and to raise them up, maybe
higher than me, definitely higher than you,
with you, and because of you.

The Breath of a House

For Halloween, I left a bucket of candy
on the front porch chair, the one there
because I remember grandfather figures
sitting in the sun to warm colding bones,
next to a shoe covered welcome mat.

The fanned pattern of slippers and shoes,
mostly browns and blacks are less Footlocker
and more a hybrid between archeological art
and searching for a favorite food
in a familiar market. It's not so much selection
as white noise. I have never understood

my White and Mexican cousins who complain
about parents and kids stealing their shoes,
and I laugh when I read Hawaiian signs saying:
Remove your shoes but no try upgrade
because to take from the trusting seems
somewhere between simple sin and hate crime.

Leaving shoes at the front of Asian homes
is like breathing to me. When asked why,
I have no cultural answer beyond my own
rationalizations and logic and questioning
why anyone would bring the outside filth
to the floors of their home. The shoe stack

out front shows the house inhale when you come
and exhale when you leave like wind traces on sand.
For Halloween, I left a bucket of candy
on the front porch filled with full-sized bars
and the thought: *if we can't have little fat nerds
of our own, we can celebrate yours with candy*

and diabetes. I had to speed Nani home
from the airport to catch the joy on her face
and the play-along questions at the sight
of straggling trick or treaters. When we returned
home, the bowl was empty, and we gasped
to feel full, even just air. The mat was bare.
The shoes were gone like someone had stolen home.

The Talk Is an Ongoing Dialogue

I never saw the looks White Mom got,
the peaking eyebrows that signal
question, comment, and concern.
I was too busy quietly begging to pick toys
instead of the arbitrary ones she'd grab
after the rush had passed on the sale rack.
Who needs three copies of Sark from *Tron*
other than the blades of a lawn mower?
It was always the least effective villains
as if she were trying to tell me *this is the best
you can hope for: middle management and evil.*

As a kid, I never saw the looks she got, but I felt
the urgency of place, and in my head I repeated
her mantra: *hands in your pockets and your pockets
in your pants* not because she thought I'd snap up
what wasn't mine but because she didn't want me
to be the target of their accusations. I never saw
the looks she got when she would turn invisible
as if her white skin was a kind of five and dime
camouflage, as if the fluorescent lights bounced
from her and spotlighted me. I never saw
the looks she got, but as a teen I learned that stockers

followed in my wake, watching.
I never saw the looks she got, but when I pick up
Mixed Nephew from school, with his darker-than-mine
skin and his curly, clipper-cut hair, I challenge
you to question, to comment, to concern. My eyes
bug out in offensive defense. I never saw the looks
White Mom got, but I am ready for them, which is, also,
part of the problem.

I Say, I Say

Mixed Nephew spits out the starting syllable of six sentences,
"Wha—duh—I—huh—woh—wha." His Foghorn Leghorn-like
stutter expresses comical surprise like his mom, Black Sister.

Every time, I shorten, but mirror, his syllabic shrapnel, conflicted
between the condition to call out the racist caricature
and the compulsion to teach him to stop because they will

judge him for this, and it's such a small thing to concede,
a loss that means next to nothing. I let my mouth quit at
"whe—nah—neh" and we laugh at the gibberish we create.

I just let him be with a kiss on the forehead, signaling
my love and blessing that he remain untouched
by my traumas a little longer.

Use the Debris to Build

I used it as extra credit bait and a reason to cancel class,
but really, I wanted to see a harbor full of dead fish,
to smell the rot of the recently asphyxiated.

The sun was out and the boardwalk shined hard
like a nephew performing Christmas magic tricks
looking for praise and approval but getting pandering;

the bars overlooking the docks were filled
with the same amount of daytime drunks
as a June gloom or full-on rainy day.

A phosphorous bloom sucked up the oxygen in the water
killing thousands of shoreline fish. The current drifted
the death-patch to shore, and the few people nearby

rushed to their destinations or choked down their midday
booze while I sat at a bench watching a mosaic of white bellies
ebb, flow, and swirl like a lead-paint-eating schizophrenic's skies.

We forget that evolution and trauma are twins
who violently break each other and use
the debris to build. We are neither stronger

nor weaker for it. Breaking and building
show the same cyclical design as one breath
to the next. Excess phosphorus killed the fish,

but it is needed to build bones. We forget that
evolution and trauma are twins who gave us
bones to break and feet to run.

Glossary of Terms
or How to Read a Christian Hanz Lozada Poem

Brown Dad: a parent who says *love* in providing and nothing more; the adjective is needed for minoritization

White Mom: a parent who says *love* in sacrifice and sometimes with words that come out as confused as skin; the adjective is needed for majoritization

Manoy: an elder, probably a brother or two, who are distinct everywhere but the page; the foreign vocabulary is needed as clue to what is lost

White Brother: a younger sibling whose lack of melanin shades his accomplishments; the adjective is needed for majoritization

White/Brown Light-skinned Aunt/Uncle: someone a little older who may or may not be related by blood but is too complicatedly connected to be a friend or acquaintance; the adjective is needed for socialization

White/Brown/Light-skinned Cousin: someone around your age who may or may not be related by blood and is too complicatedly connected to be a friend or acquaintance; the adjective is needed for socialization

White/Black/Brown Brother/Sister: someone who may or may not be a sibling but is too complicatedly connected to be a cousin, friend, or acquaintance; the adjective is needed for socialization

Mixed/White/Yellow Nephew: someone who is younger than you who may or may not be related by blood and is too complicatedly connected to be just some kid; the adjective is needed for socialization

Monster: the author of the poem when he feels separated by skin; no adjective should be needed for socialization; the world does it

Nani: a woman who is too complex to be described in crude terms; no adjective is used

Individuals: names are worthless when the tongue stumbles easily

Afterforeword

I think this might be a good one.

I receive the text at 6:30 AM while reading a Philip K. Dick novel, an Eduardo Galeano history, or a Barbara Jane Reyes poetry collection, anything rather than focusing on my own writing. We never exchanged texts before I moved to San Francisco. We would meet at least a couple times a month in a coffee shop in Long Beach, the middle point between our residences. Whatever we had to say could wait. Whatever work we wanted to show each other could wait. Distance changes dynamics. The text exchanges occur almost daily. It's not that there is more urgency now, it's that the middle has expanded to encompass the greater space between. To meet there has become easier but requires greater deliberation. Christian's words are more deliberate and travel farther.

Lightning strikes in many shapes and patterns. Perhaps it is like a snowflake.

When Lozada turned from the novels of his early days as a writer to focus his attention on poetry, he drifted along in the river of words, ramming into the banks, arriving at broken yet beautiful docks. He is now in full control of the rudder, weaving among the islets with precision, and determining when to break the docks and when to break the boat.

> "But the child was hers – a living bridge between two worlds.
> Let people talk."
> — Langston Hughes, *The Ways of White Folks*

He's a Color Until He's Not represents a journey of growth, a poet learning to negotiate with himself and the, often, harsh world around him. It's a coming to terms with Filipino identity, then with white identity, and finally navigating the broken, fragmented territory that those of singular-presenting ethnicities lay at the feet of the mixed-race.

We focus so much on the fact that each snowflake is unique that we sometimes forget they are all snowflakes, and that when we look at the peak of the mountain in winter, we see snow.

"When it is genuine, when it is born of the need to speak, no one can stop the human voice. When denied a mouth, it speaks with the hands or the eyes, or the pores, or anything at all. Because every single one of us has something to say to the others, something that deserves to be celebrated or forgiven by others."
— Eduardo Galeano, *The Book of Embraces*

The middle way is not just a Buddhist approach.

Lozada's poetry begins with himself then extends outward, holding out a hand to humanity, showing compassion for the rest of us when our compassion rather should be directed toward him but for our gross misunderstanding of what it means to live in the middle.

The lightning will pass before you realize it's there. A single snowflake is a thing of beauty. So too is the snow.

— Steven Hendrix

About the Author

Christian Hanz Lozada is the son of an immigrant Filipino and a descendant of the Confederacy. His heart beats with hope and exclusion. He co-authored the poetry book *Leave with More Than You Came With* from Arroyo Seco Press and the history book *Hawaiian in Los Angeles*. His poems and stories have appeared in *Hawaii Pacific Review* (Pushcart Nominee), *A&U Magazine, Rigorous Journal, Cultural Weekly, Dryland, Pilgrimage Press*, among others. Christian has featured at the Autry Museum, the Twin Towers Correctional Facility, Tebot Bach, and Beyond Baroque. He lives in San Pedro, CA, and uses his MFA to teach his neighbors' kids at Los Angeles Harbor College.

Acknowledgments

Thanks to all the editors of journals and anthologies who published versions of the poems in this book. Y'all got an eye:

82, Dryland, Drunk Monkeys, Another New Calligraphy, Cultural Daily, Hawai'i Pacific Review, Marias at Sampaguitas, Pilgrimage Press, Rigorous Journal, and *Rush.*

Thank you to my parents who raised me to be observant and paranoid. I wouldn't see the world so dark and light without these skills.

Thanks to Grandma who taught me how to love, even if it cuts.

My gratitude to my brothers for the laughs, the anger, and the never seeing the right version of me.

Thank you to my partner, "Do you know who the fuck I am" Lessa Kanani'opua Pelayo-Lozada, in all things whether she wants it. Even if you disagree, you still back my play and give me space to learn.

Thank you to Steven Hendrix for the beautiful afterword and reading too many of these poems too many times in too many versions even though we haven't occupied the same room in years.

Thank you to my students who show me every year what aspirational capital means.

Thank you to the kids I'll never have and never unintentionally traumatize and never lift above the generational trauma even though I share every parent's mad desire to try.

Also Available from Moon Tide Press

The Language of Fractions, Nicelle Davis (2023)
Paradise Anonymous, Oriana Ivy (2023)
Now You Are a Missing Person, Susan Hayden (2023)
Maze Mouth, Brian Sonia-Wallace (2023)
Tangled by Blood, Rebecca Evans (2023)
Another Way of Loving Death, Jeremy Ra (2023)
Kissing the Wound, J.D. Isip (2023)
Feed It to the River, Terhi K. Cherry (2022)
Beat Not Beat: An Anthology of California Poets Screwing on the Beat and Post-Beat Tradition (2022)
When There Are Nine: Poems Celebrating the Life an Achievements of Ruth Bader Ginsburg (2022)
The Knife Thrower's Daughter, Terri Niccum (2022)
2 Revere Place, Aruni Wijesinghe (2022)
Here Go the Knives, Kelsey Bryan-Zwick (2022)
Trumpets in the Sky, Jerry Garcia (2022)
Threnody, Donna Hilbert (2022)
A Burning Lake of Paper Suns, Ellen Webre (2021)
Instructions for an Animal Body, Kelly Gray (2021)
Head *V* Heart: New & Selected Poems, Rob Sturma (2021)
Sh!t Men Say to Me: A Poetry Anthology in Response to Toxic Masculinity (2021)
Flower Grand First, Gustavo Hernandez (2021)
Everything is Radiant Between the Hates, Rich Ferguson (2020)
When the Pain Starts: Poetry as Sequential Art, Alan Passman (2020)
This Place Could Be Haunted If I Didn't Believe in Love, Lincoln McElwee (2020)
Impossible Thirst, Kathryn de Lancellotti (2020)
Lullabies for End Times, Jennifer Bradpiece (2020)
Crabgrass World, Robin Axworthy (2020)
Contortionist Tongue, Dania Ayah Alkhouli (2020)
The only thing that makes sense is to grow, Scott Ferry (2020)
Dead Letter Box, Terri Niccum (2019)
Tea and Subtitles: Selected Poems 1999-2019, Michael Miller (2019)
At the Table of the Unknown, Alexandra Umlas (2019)

The Book of Rabbits, Vince Trimboli (2019)
Everything I Write Is a Love Song to the World, David McIntire (2019)
Letters to the Leader, HanaLena Fennel (2019)
Darwin's Garden, Lee Rossi (2019)
Dark Ink: A Poetry Anthology Inspired by Horror (2018)
Drop and Dazzle, Peggy Dobreer (2018)
Junkie Wife, Alexis Rhone Fancher (2018)
The Moon, My Lover, My Mother, & the Dog, Daniel McGinn (2018)
Lullaby of Teeth: An Anthology of Southern California Poetry (2017)
Angels in Seven, Michael Miller (2016)
A Likely Story, Robbi Nester (2014)
Embers on the Stairs, Ruth Bavetta (2014)
The Green of Sunset, John Brantingham (2013)
The Savagery of Bone, Timothy Matthew Perez (2013)
The Silence of Doorways, Sharon Venezio (2013)
Cosmos: An Anthology of Southern California Poetry (2012)
Straws and Shadows, Irena Praitis (2012)
In the Lake of Your Bones, Peggy Dobreer (2012)
I Was Building Up to Something, Susan Davis (2011)
Hopeless Cases, Michael Kramer (2011)
One World, Gail Newman (2011)
What We Ache For, Eric Morago (2010)
Now and Then, Lee Mallory (2009)
Pop Art: An Anthology of Southern California Poetry (2009)
In the Heaven of Never Before, Carine Topal (2008)
A Wild Region, Kate Buckley (2008)
Carving in Bone: An Anthology of Orange County Poetry (2007)
Kindness from a Dark God, Ben Trigg (2007)
A Thin Strand of Lights, Ricki Mandeville (2006)
Sleepyhead Assassins, Mindy Nettifee (2006)
Tide Pools: An Anthology of Orange County Poetry (2006)
Lost American Nights: Lyrics & Poems, Michael Ubaldini (2006)

Patrons

Moon Tide Press would like to thank the following people for their support in helping publish the finest poetry from the Southern California region. To sign up as a patron, visit www.moontidepress.com or send an email to publisher@moontidepress.com.

Anonymous
Robin Axworthy
Conner Brenner
Nicole Connolly
Bill Cushing
Susan Davis
Kristen Baum DeBeasi
Peggy Dobreer
Kate Gale
Dennis Gowans
Alexis Rhone Fancher
HanaLena Fennel
Half Off Books & Brad T. Cox
Donna Hilbert
Jim & Vicky Hoggatt
Michael Kramer
Ron Koertge & Bianca Richards
Gary Jacobelly
Ray & Christi Lacoste
Jeffery Lewis
Zachary & Tammy Locklin
Lincoln McElwee
David McIntire
José Enrique Medina
Michael Miller & Rachanee Srisavasdi
Michelle & Robert Miller
Ronny & Richard Morago
Terri Niccum
Andrew November
Jeremy Ra
Luke & Mia Salazar
Jennifer Smith
Roger Sponder
Andrew Turner
Rex Wilder
Mariano Zaro
Wes Bryan Zwick

www.ingramcontent.com/pod-product-compliance
Lightning Source LLC
Chambersburg PA
CBHW031138090426
42738CB00008B/1141